When Life

Doesn't

Make Sense

by
Fr. Joseph Breighner

Edited by
Judith Dobler

Cathedral Foundation Press

Printed and bound in the United States of America

1 2 3 4 5   06 05 04 03 02 01 00 99 98 97

ISBN 1-885938-08-X

Library of Congress Catalog Card Number: 97-66561

Published in 1997 by

Cathedral Foundation Press
P.O. Box 777
Baltimore, Maryland 21203

Publisher: Daniel L. Medinger
Assistant Manager: Patti Medinger
Book and cover design: Sue Seiler

❧ *Author's Note* ❧

This book is intended to help people understand, and heal from, the tragedies and losses of life. "If God is for us, who can be against us?" perhaps best summarizes my intent.

Unfortunately, when we have experienced some terrible tragedy, we often have a hard time believing that there is a God, much less that this God is on our side. I hope this book will help you to understand how I believe God works.

If you find this book helpful to you, please encourage others to read it. If you find yourself in disagreement with part or all of this book, then just let it be. While I hope that this work will help you to think differently about God, I'm not interested in polemics or battles. The mystery of God is so great, and the reality of evil is so perplexing, that no one book, especially a small book like this, can hope to say all that there is to say about either God or evil.

To help you to understand the make up of the book, you will note that at the end of each chapter I have included a "meditation" from some other source.

Many reflections and meditations come across my desk constantly. Often I do not know their origins. Throughout the book I have identified as many as possible.

I especially want to thank the many people involved in producing this book: Mike and Helen Eder, my sister and brother-in-law, for their early encouragement and editing; Judy Dobler for her help in getting this book into its final form; Dan Medinger and the Cathedral Foundation Press for deciding to publish it; and all the support staff at the press and at the Baltimore *Catholic Review*.

Since this book aims to help us to cope with and heal from the

tragedies of life, I want to dedicate this book to models of cop-
ing and healing.

First, I want to dedicate this book
to Craig and Susan Warnick and
their five-year-old daughter,
Chloe. Craig battled brain tumors
for twenty years of his life, and
Susan stayed faithfully by his
side all that time, until his death
in January 1997. I have a whole
essay on the Warnicks in the "ad-
ditional readings" section of this
book. I will contribute a portion
of my royalties to: The Chloe
Warnick Education Fund, P.O.
Box 4684, Timonium, MD 21094-
4684.

Second, I dedicate this book to the work of Catholic Relief Services, who serve the poorest of the poor in over 85 countries around the world. They base their services on "need, not creed." To assist them in their worldwide task of caring, I will donate part of my royalties to them as well.

If you would care to be a part of their ongoing development programs, as well as their emergency assistance programs, you may donate to: Catholic Relief Services, P.O. Box 17090, Baltimore, MD 21203.

∿ Introduction ∿

When Life Doesn't Make Sense

Loss is a part of life. We live knowing we will die. An old saying used to go, "The only two things in life that you have to do are pay taxes and die." Throughout history, many people have attempted, with varying degrees of success, to cheat the tax man. No one has successfully cheated death! Shortly before I began work on this book I saw a news story about the oldest man in China who had just died at the age of 147. He lived about twice as long as the average person, but still death claimed him.

Beyond struggling with our personal mortality, we also face times in life when the tragedies of life seem as though they will overwhelm us — the death of a child, the loss of a spouse or parent, a terrible accident, a life threatening illness, auto and plane crashes, wars and famines, ethnic cleansing and concentration camps. The list could go on.

In those darkest moments we wonder whether faith in God is any more than a cruel illusion. We hear others ask, and we ask ourselves, the perennial question,

"How can a good God let this happen?" The question behind all our questions is "Where is God?"

This is not the first book to attempt to wrestle with the question of how there can be a good God in a world filled with so much evil. Most likely this will not be the last book to attempt to deal with the problem of evil. Rabbi Harold Kushner's book *When Bad Things Happen To Good People* and the Rev. Lesley Weatherhead's *The Will Of God* are two books that have helped me immensely with my own reflections on the problem of good and evil. I will borrow heavily from *The Will of God.*

When Life Doesn't Make Sense is divided into three parts:

The first section is on the will of God. Since my conclusion from that section is that God wills only good things, the next section follows logically.

The second section deals with the question, "Where do evil and sickness and death come from?"

The third section addresses the question, "Where is God when tragedy and death occur?"

While I will struggle with the whole mystery of evil, this is not a mystery book. I don't mind telling you my conclusion right up front.

I believe it is never God's will for the baby to die, for the tragedy to happen, for the plane to crash. As I will show in the chapters ahead, I believe God always intends good for us, that he shares our pain with us, and that he will see to it that we even triumph over death in the ultimate defeat of evil.

I have had my own personal tragedies and losses in my life, and I have stayed by others as they experienced far greater tragedies and losses. My faith has been battered but not shattered. I have emerged from some dark moments in my own life.

My hope is that this book will help you believe that as you experience the dark valleys in your life, you will discover that God did not put you in the darkness, but like the Good Shepherd he is, God is carrying you out of the darkness and into the light.

Section One

❧

The Will of God

Chapter One

∾

God's Intentional Will

Faced with the tragedies of life, how do we understand the will of God? Is it God's will that the baby dies, the train wrecks, the bridge collapses? Hardly. We would put in jail anyone who would deliberately kill a child, cause a train to derail or a bridge to fall! Such people would be labeled child killers or terrorists! How could we ever worship or praise a God who would do such things when we punish people who do those things?

The theological problem for many of us is that we lack sufficient distinctions, the right words, to explain the workings of God. Since a central part of our Jewish-Christian tradition is to see God's will as ultimately controlling human history, it would seem that God must be the source of the bad things as well as the good things.

Job articulated this understanding in the Bible when he spoke these profound words:

"The Lord gives and the Lord takes away. Blessed be the name of the Lord."

Job was right in attributing the good to God. He was wrong in blaming God for the bad. Even the book of Job clearly pictures Satan (my subject for a later chapter) as the cause of Job's misery, not God. God goes along with the test and ultimately rewards Job's faith, but God does not do the damage.

To understand God's will more practically, I am forever indebted to the Rev. Lesley Weatherhead's presentation. He pictures God's will under three headings, three understandings.

First, there is God's *intentional will*, what God intends to happen.

Second, there is God's *circumstantial will* — how the circumstances of life attempt to alter God's plan.

Third, and finally, there is God's *ultimate will* — how God ultimately triumphs over evil, brokenness, sin, and death.

Let's look at those three wills separately.

First, God's *intentional will* is always for good. God always intends for good things to happen. The earliest pages of the Bible picture God creating everything and seeing that it is good. God then creates man and woman in his own image! God gives our first parents a wonderful garden to live in. That Adam and Eve manage, through their pride and willfulness, to even mess up the Garden of Eden is a recognition of human perversity, not to God's doing or wanting anything bad to happen.

In the Christian belief system, God sends a Savior, his own son Jesus. Again, the intention is always for good. The Father sends the Son not only to atone for sin, but to teach us a whole new way to live: to love, not hate; to forgive, not seek revenge; to serve, not dominate; to give away what we have to help those who have less, not to amass vast fortunes; to build a world based on peace and justice, not based on power and cruelty. The intention of the Father is for good. It is to recreate us again in the image and likeness of God and to recreate the good world God created.

And all that Jesus did was good. That's why my heart always breaks when I hear people glibly refer to some tragedy as "God's will." No doubt they mean to be helpful, but the image of God they portray is so hurtful! Years ago I recall watching the national news on TV and hearing a story about a bus loaded with school children that had gone over the edge of a cliff. Many of the children were injured; some were killed. And there, right on national television, was one of the school's religion teachers saying, "Oh, it was God's will!" I just wanted to crawl right inside the television and get to her and say, No, no, God doesn't do stuff like that! Come look at this Jesus and see what he did.

He didn't take able-bodied people and disable them; he found the disabled and made them well again.

He didn't take seeing people and blind them; he found blind people and helped them to see.

He didn't take hearing people and burst their eardrums; he found deaf people and gave them hearing.

He didn't take healthy people and make them sick; he took sick people and made them healthy again.

He didn't kill people; he found dead people and raised them to life. Life and wholeness and health and healing and goodness: These are God's Will.

God doesn't kill and injure children. If King Herod, who did slaughter the infants in an effort to kill Jesus, if Herod had been

God, then I would have to agree that God must kill kids. But Herod was not the hero of the New Testament. Jesus was.

Jesus was a *victim* of evil, a *victim* of fear and narrow-mindedness, a *victim* of human cruelty. Jesus was never the *cause* of any of these things!

Yes, I do believe that great good can come about as a result of terrible tragedies. Yes, people with disabilities and sicknesses and limitations of various kinds are often able to triumph over such realities and become inspirations for millions. But these are examples of God's presence comforting and strengthening people in times of trial, not God causing the trial! To name the tragedy as the will of God is to make God appear indifferent at best, and sadistic, at worst.

To name God as the good God, as the one who intends good for all in every circumstance of life, is to accurately name God.

And if we're honest, good outweighs evil thousands of times every day. Yes, the news is filled with stories of death and destruction and murder and rape and terrorism. But these grab the headlines because they are still the exception! Good is still the norm. Now if we start seeing headlines like:

Boy hugs dog or
Teacher helps student
we'd better start worrying because it would mean that good
had become the exception!

So God's *intentional will* for good
is all around us in

> the beauty of the sunrise
>   or sunset,
> a child's smile,
> a couple in love,
> a family at play,
> a medical professional
>   at work,
> a good teacher in the
>   classroom,
> a person at prayer,
> and on and on.

If we stopped to name all the good things that happened to us on any given day, from the food we ate, to the chair we sat on, to the person who smiled at us in the mall — if we named all the thousands of things we take for granted each day, we would see so much more good.

So, God's *intentional will* is for good, not evil. And goodness is all around us. But sadness and death and tragedy are also a part of life. So after a brief meditation let's move on to look at God's *circumstantial will*, how the "circumstances of life" alter and affect God's will, at least in the short run.

God's Intentional Will
A Meditation

∾

God's Plan

Many of us hear words about "God's plan" for us. But what does that mean? Allow me to share the following reflection with you:

God has a plan for me. It is hidden within me ("the kingdom of God is within you"), just as the oak is hidden within the acorn or the rose within the bud. As I yield myself more fully to God, his plan expresses itself more perfectly through me. I can tell when I am in tune with it for then my mind and heart are filled with a deep inner peace. This peace fills me with a sense of security, with the desire and joy to take the steps that are part of the plan.

God's plan for me is a perfect part of a larger plan. It is designed for the good of all and not for me alone. It is a many-sided plan and reaches out through all the people I meet. All the events and people who come into my life are instruments for unfolding this plan.

God has chosen those people whom he wants me to know, to love, and to serve. We are continually being drawn to one another in ways that are not coincidental. I pray that I may become a better instrument to love and serve and that I may become more worthy to receive the love and service of others.

I ask God for only those things he wants me to have. I know that these benefits will come to me at the right time and in the right way. This inner knowing frees my mind and heart from greed, jealousy, anger, and resentment. It gives me the courage and faith to do those things I feel are mine to do. I no longer look with envy at what others are receiving, nor do I compare myself with them. Therefore, I do not cut myself off from God, the giver of all good things.

God's gifts to me can be many times greater than I am now receiving. I pray that I may increase my capacity to give, for I can give only as I receive and receive only as I give. I believe that when I cannot do those things I desire to do, it is because I have not seen or heard God's guidance. It is then that God uses the trouble or apparent failure that may result to help me face myself and see the new opportunity before me.

The real purpose of my life is to find God and help my fellow men and women. I thank God for each experience that helps me surrender myself to his will. For only as I lose myself in the consciousness of God's presence can his plan for my life be fulfilled.

Chapter 2

∾

God's Circumstantial Will

If it is the intention of God that all be good, as I contend it is, then the next logical question is

Where did all the bad come from?

What happens to God's good intentions is what happens when the will of God meets opposition. These are what I call the "circumstances of life" that attempt to alter or obstruct God's will. I will

go into detail about each of these
in the second section of this book
where I discuss the question,
"Where do evil and sickness and
death come from?"

To give you a sneak preview, I list
four categories of opposition to
God's will:

1) *The spirit of evil,* which we tra-
ditionally name the devil.

2) *Original Sin,* which means we
inherit the brokenness of our first
parents, our tendency in life to
miss making the right decision.

3) *Free Will,* which means that we
humans are "free," that we have
the ability to be people who

choose life or choose death, that we can become people who choose to give life and love to others or who inflict death and hate on others.

4) *The forces of nature,* which means that God ordinarily respects the laws of his own c r e a - tion. For example, a bus going over a cliff will inflict terrible damage on the occupants of the bus.

These are the circumstances that alter or impede the will of God in the short run. Since I'll devote an entire chapter to each one later in the book, allow me to use just two examples of what I mean.

First, a very human analogy. All

healthy parents and grandparents have wonderful intentions for their children or grandchildren. They want each child to be healthy and happy, to do well in school and in life, to be successful, caring, and giving.

So, let's say, for example, that you want your child to be a butcher, a baker, a candlestick maker, a doctor, a lawyer, a priest. But then, God forbid, let's say that a war breaks out somewhere in the world, and we become embroiled in another worldwide conflict. Then suppose your child or grandchild comes to you and says, "Mom, Dad, Grandma, and Grandpa, I no longer want to be a candlestick maker. I want to join the military. I want to help end the conflict. I want to protect those women from being raped, those children from being killed, those men from continuing to be slaughtered."

Now, under those circumstances, your original intention for your child did not come true. However, ultimately you probably are not too disappointed. Your son or daughter, grandson or granddaughter is still a caring person, someone willing to help others, even willing to risk his or her life to do so. So your *ultimate will* (my theme for the next chapter) is not frustrated. While the child did

not fulfill your specific intention,
the child still has become a good
person.

Now, let's alter my example. Let's
say that you had the same good
intentions for your child or
grandchild, but that he or she
"got in with the wrong crowd" or
was addicted to drugs or became
a criminal. Clearly, in this case,
your good intentions, your love
and care and energy, were sabo-
taged by the circumstances of life.
Tragically, this happens every
day to humans. Parents have broken hearts over dreams for their
children that did not come true or
over potential greatness that was
never realized.

However, if you are a person of faith, my three-part model of God's will (the *intentional*, the *circumstantial*, and the *ultimate will*) can be of enormous comfort. God's will can be altered and delayed, but never ultimately stopped. Now, maybe you are thinking, *What do you mean? My son was killed. My daughter committed suicide. My son killed someone. How can you say it will ultimately work out?*

Our faith tells us that God makes all things work together for good because we believe in life after death. The dead do live in eternity, and even the most tragic events can have positive side ef-

fects. One person's death may inspire others to get out of drugs.
One person's suicide may inspire
someone else to become a coun-
selor who works with depressed
people. No pain is ever wasted.
No human misery is ever without
its redemptive quality. From a
purely human point of view,
something may seem absolutely
absurd. From God's point of
view, nothing is ever lost forever.

So I would hope that parents and
grandparents and aunts and un-
cles who have great intentions for
their children and grandchildren,
for their nieces and nephews,
would find peace in this three-
part image of God's *will*.

All we can do is put our best into those we love. We can control our intentions. However, we have no control over the circumstances of life, including the choices of our adult children. At some point we have to let God be God and experience the peace that comes from believing that ultimately all will work out. We humans only see from the perspective of a few decades of life. God sees from the perspective of infinite years.

Now, let's take a giant step up and see all of this from God's perspective. As I said before, we Christians believe that God sent his son Jesus to redeem us, to teach us a whole new way to live.

God's intention was not to kill his son! This would make God a cruel and blood-letting person. God's intention was to send his son to be a faithful witness to his Father.

Perhaps the Gospel story that most captures the *intentional* and *circumstantial will* of the Father is the story of the vineyard owner who wanted his share of the grapes from his tenants.

First, the Gospel tells us, the owner sent his servants to the tenants to demand his share. Some of these servants were beaten; others were killed.

Then the master said, "I will send my son. Surely they will respect him."

But they did not respect the son in the parable or in the real life story of Jesus. The son was killed.

Put simply, because of the set of circumstances that Jesus found himself in, he knew that if he were faithful to the *intention* of his Father, he would die on a cross.

Jesus knew that if he continued to speak of God as his Father, the religious leaders of his day would accuse him of blasphemy.

He knew that if he continued to cure people on the Sabbath, to show that a human person was more sacred than human law, he would be condemned as a law-breaker.

He knew that if he continued to preach the goodness of God to the marginal people of his day — the women, the tax collectors, the poor and the outcast, he would be accused of disturbing and confusing the people.

Jesus knew that if he ate and drank with sinners, he would be accused of being a drunkard and a glutton.

To put it simply, to be faithful to the Father's *intention*, Jesus knew the cross would be the *circumstantial will* of the Father. Again, here is the key: God the Father did not put Jesus on a cross or will his death. That happened as a result of the stubbornness of some religious leaders, the fears and jealousy of others, the fickleness of the crowds, and the pettiness of civil government.

It would be hard for us to imagine worse circumstances in which to end a human life. Jesus was rejected by the religious leaders of his day, executed by the civil leaders, abandoned by his friends, misunderstood by his own family.

The intention of the Father had been for Jesus to redeem us and to teach us how to live in love and harmony and to create a society built on peace and justice. The circumstances of the times were such that Jesus was "ambushed" by the very evil he had sought to conquer, killed by the people he had hoped to save, misunderstood by a world that he had fallen in love with.

But the circumstances of life would not win. Jesus modeled such faith in his Father that his followers would forever know to never give up. When all seems lost in the circumstances of life, faith tells us to remember God's good intentions and God's ultimate victory. The circumstances of life could not defeat Jesus. They will not defeat us. The greatest miracle had not yet been worked. The ultimate victory was yet to be won.

God's Circumstantial Will
A Meditation

∽

Welcome to Holland

We all live with many disappointments in life. Parents who have children with disabilities often experience an acute sense of pain. There's a little parable that I came across, however, that helps put things in perspective. It's entitled *Welcome to Holland* and the author is Emily Pearl Kingsley.

People often ask me to describe the experience of raising a child with a disability to try to help people who have not shared that unique experience to understand it, to imagine how it would feel. It's like this:

When you're going to have a baby, it's like planning a fabulous vacation trip to Italy. You buy a bunch of guidebooks and make your wonderful plans — the Coliseum, Michelangelo's David, the gondolas in Venice. You may learn some handy phrases in Italian. It's all very exciting.

After months of eager anticipation, the day finally arrives. You pack your bags and off you go. Several hours later, the plane lands. The flight attendant says, "Welcome to Holland!"

"Holland?" you ask. "What do you mean, Holland? I signed up for Italy! I'm supposed to be in Italy. All my life I've dreamed of going to Italy."

But there's been a change in the flight plan. They've landed in Holland, and there you must stay. The important thing is that they haven't taken you to a horrible, disgusting, filthy place full of pestilence, famine, and disease: It's just a different place.

So you must go out and buy new guide books. And you must learn a whole new language. And you meet a whole new group of people you would never have met in Italy.

It's just a different place. It's slower paced than Italy, less flashy than

Italy. But after you've been there awhile and catch your breath, you look around and you begin to notice that Holland has windmills. Holland has tulips. Holland even has Rembrandts.

But everyone you know is busy coming and going from Italy, and they're all bragging about what a wonderful time they had there. And for the rest of your life, you will say, "Yes, that's where I was supposed to go. That's what I had planned."

And the pain of that will never, ever go away because the loss of that dream is a very significant loss. But if you spend the rest of your life mourning the fact that you didn't get to Italy, you may never be free to en-

joy the very special, the very lovely things about Holland.

Chapter Three

∾

God's Ultimate Will

God cannot be defeated. God always intends good for his creatures and his creation. Circumstances can interfere with God's intentions. Circumstances can even appear to have defeated God's plan or to have destroyed God as witnessed in Jesus' death on the cross.

But something happened three days after that crucifixion and death. The tomb was empty. The body was gone. Jesus was alive again. Orthodox Christians celebrate Easter, picturing the devil as the original April Fool. When it appeared that he had defeated goodness and Godness, suddenly there was Easter. There was God alive again. There was the triumph of goodness over evil. There was the victory of light over darkness.

The *ultimate will* of God is nothing less than the absolute trust that God will always prevail. It is a trust based on absolute faith.

"Seeing is believing" is how most of us Americans approach life.

But "believing is seeing" is how the believer approaches life.

Faith gives us a lens, a way to view life, a way to trust the basic goodness of life.

I realize that some people reading this book may not have such faith. Faith is God's gift, not mine. However, God will give faith to those who honestly search for it, who open themselves to God's gracious presence. While I cannot give faith, I can offer my reasons for trusting in God's ultimate triumph.

First, I believe in the resurrection of Jesus from the dead because I find the first witnesses of that event to be credible people. To put it simply, it is very clear from the Gospels that the early followers of Jesus did not always believe in him while he was alive. If they were conflicted in their belief while Jesus was alive and active, why would they suddenly put their faith in a dead man?

And their faith in this Jesus, alive again, did not win them honor, prestige, or fame. It brought them persecution, rejection, dishonor, and ultimately exile and death. If their intent was to fabricate a lie, it's hard to imagine that they would have gone to such lengths to do it.

Interestingly, too, is that recent scholarship reveals that there were many people similar to Jesus at that time. There were miracle workers, magicians as they were called then, some of whom even claimed to be the Messiah. But other than as footnotes in scholarly research, we know nothing about them.

There had to be something different about this Jesus, something as wonderful as rising from the dead, for him to have died with virtually no followers, and now, two thousand years later, to have over a billion followers worldwide. No, numbers alone do not prove anything, but they can imply some compelling force that gives belief real credibility.

Second, I believe in God's ultimate triumph, in the ultimate victory of God's will, because it is the only belief that gives meaning to life. If there is no life after death, then life has no meaning. All that we learn, accomplish, and achieve is obliterated by death. How can a world that is guided by order, a world of seasons following seasons, of laws of physics and chemistry, always hold true? How can such order have come from nothing?

To look at it another way, what sense would it make for an

Adolph Hitler and a Mother Teresa of Calcutta to have the same destiny? Hitler used his life to bring death to millions of Jews and Christians and brought havoc and destruction to countless people. Should his life have the same reward — just rotting in the grave — as Mother Teresa who has used her life to bring life to all religions, all nations, all peoples? And Mother Teresa is very clear that she would not do what she does except for her faith in the risen Lord, except for her daily awareness of this Lord in her life, except for an absolute conviction that there is life after death!

While various people throughout history have found ways to pervert Christianity, to use it for their own financial or personal gain, the solid witness of true believers always transcends the failures of others. There can be various reasons why a person may fail to be a good Christian, but there can be only one reason why a person would give up everything to follow Christ. And that is an absolute faith in the resurrection of Christ from the dead.

No, I'm not saying that each person must be a Christian or a Catholic to be saved. I'm simply saying that if you follow your conscience, if you seek God with a sincere heart, you will find God and you will know that God's will ultimately triumphs.

The ultimate victory, however, is just that, ultimate, final. On a day-to-day basis, there is great resistance to love, to truth, to beauty, to peace, to goodness. The circumstances of life continually oppose the intention of God. What is this force that opposes God? If God always intends life and love and goodness, then where do sin and sickness and death come from? Let's look at these questions as we move to the second section of this book.

God's Ultimate Will
A Meditation

❧

Three Trees

*T*hree trees grew next to one another in the forest and shared
with each other their dreams of what
they would become.

The first tree said, "I dream of becoming part of a luxurious home
where many famous people come and
go and admire the grain and color of
my wood."

The second tree said, "My dream is to become the tall mast of an elegant ship that sails the seven seas."

The third tree said, "My dream is to become part of a great tower, so high that it will inspire people who look at it. People will come from all over to see it."

And so the three trees dreamed. Eventually they grew to maturity and were cut down. The first didn't become a part of a luxurious home as it had dreamed. Instead some of its wood was fashioned into a simple manger, a wooden trough to hold the hay that animals ate.

The second tree didn't become the tall mast of an elegant ship as it had

dreamed but rather the sides of an or-
dinary fishing boat like so many others on the Sea of Galilee.

The third didn't become part of a tall
tower as it had dreamed but was
fashioned into the beams of a cross
and used for crucifixion.

A great parable, isn't it? You and I
may not have our dreams come true.
But if you and I believe in God, we
know that God will bring greater
dreams to our lives.

Section Two

❧

Where Do Evil, Sin, and Death Come From?

Chapter Four

∽

The Spirit of Evil

Hopefully by now, I have established that the intention of God is always for good, that the "circumstances" of life resist and alter that intention, but that God's *ultimate will* prevails in the end. The next logical questions then are:

Where do these circumstances come from?

If God created the world good, then why is there anything that is not good in the world?

Good questions. Challenging questions. Let's attempt to answer them by looking at the four apparent causes of evil, sin, and death.

First, the chief opponent to God is what we could call simply the Spirit of Evil. There are various names for this entity: the Devil, Lucifer, Beelzebub, the Prince of Darkness, Lord of the Flies, Satan, Father of Lies, and so on.

From earliest times, from biblical texts and church tradition, the devil is understood to be a fallen angel. Again, a creature of God's *intentional will* would be good. However, a creature created by God with free will can exercise that will, even to oppose God. Thus Lucifer became a fallen angel, an agent of darkness rather than an agent of light. He became the force opposed to God, the leader of other fallen angels.

In our sophisticated age, I realize that that summary explanation of the devil seems simple and childlike. I agree. However, it also does not mean such a concept is not true.

My purpose here is not to argue about the existence of the devil or

even to debate how the devil
should be pictured. A creature
with pointed ears and an evil face
and a pitchfork may or may not
appeal to you. But I do contend
that there is a reality, a spiritual
entity that opposes good.

A simple but sincere person once
said, "If you want proof of the
devil's existence, just try to do
something good." Note how hard
it is to do that on a consistent basis. This "opposition" to goodness was proof enough for this
person that an evil force exists.

Psychology often has a difficult
time with the devil. Too often the
devil is seen simply as a projec-
tion of our inner darkness on

someone outside ourselves in order to avoid responsibility for our own decisions. "The devil made me do it" can be a way to avoid personal responsibility and to blame someone else for our actions.

However, while psychology may alert us to our own inner darkness, our "dark side," it can in no way disprove the existence of a personal entity that works against God and goodness in us and around us.

In fact, life itself seems to point to evil incarnate. When we look at the terrible atrocities of life — the avoidable famine in Somalia, the senseless slaughter in Rwanda and in the former Yugoslavia, at the concentrations camps of the Nazis, at the cruelties of all human history — we see evil on such a grand scale that a spirit of evil becomes quite believable.

However we choose to understand this force, clearly this is the source of death and destruction. When insurance companies call hurricanes and tornadoes and other natural disasters "acts of God," I wonder what God they know or believe in. "Acts of the Devil" seems a far better description. Jesus said that he came that we might have "life and life to the fullest." He said he would give us a "joy that no one could take from us." He promised a "peace that the world cannot give." That doesn't sound like a God of earthquakes or hurricanes. These sound far more like the work of an evil spirit.

In addition to being a great opposing force that glories in death, disease, destruction, and disasters, the devil also takes on a very specific role in relation to human beings. The devil becomes the great tempter, the seducer, the one who leads us into sin and death.

I recall the story of the newly married couple who had just worked out a very tight budget.

The next day the young wife happened to pass a clothing store, saw a great outfit reduced 80 percent, and bought it.

When she returned home, her husband was not amused.

"Honey," he said, "we can't afford anything right now. Why did you buy it?"

His wife replied, "The devil made me do it."

The husband retorted, "Then why didn't you do what Jesus did and say, 'Get thee behind me, Satan?'"

The wife replied, "I did, and the devil said, 'That outfit looks great from the back too.'"

One of the best descriptions of the devil at work was given by the great radio and television personality, Bishop Fulton J. Sheen. Bishop Sheen said that before we sin, the devil is the "great excuser." He gives us all the excuses:

"You're tired; have a drink."
"Your wife will never find out."
"Take the money; no one will notice."

After we sin, the devil becomes the "great accuser." He shames us: "Look what you did, you no good slime-ball, you *sinner!*"

Consequently, I always try to make an important distinction between guilt and shame.

Guilt says, "I did a bad thing," and guilt can be appropriate.

Shame says, "I am a bad person," and shame is never appropriate.

We can do bad things for which we need to repent, make restitution, and try to do better. What we do, however, is not who we are! We will always be children of God, people made in God's image and likeness, people God loves with an everlasting love. No matter what we do, we never lose that identity. That's why the church must always be an instrument of forgiveness and healing.

Shame is the work of the devil keeping people away from God and forgiveness.

Forgiveness is the work of God and of God's people.

What does the work of the devil mean practically? Well, to pick up on the example of the school bus accident: The devil may have said to the driver, "Come on. You can drive a little faster. You'll get home quicker."

Or the spirit of evil could have said to the mechanic who serviced the bus, "Don't take all that time to put new brakes on the bus. These will be okay for a while."

Or maybe the devil tempted the engineer who designed the road, "Hey, so what if that curve is a little dangerous. Most cars will slow down. Don't spend all that time and money redesigning it."

Do you get the point? The temptation to be less than what we might be, to be less than excellent people and to do less than excellent work, to give in to our sloth and our lust, this is all the work of the spirit of evil. Having free will, we are free to listen to the spirit of evil rather than listen to our consciences, which are the voice of the Spirit of God within us.

So the devil is the key force opposing God, the key in a set of life circumstances that attempt to obstruct God's will. But there's more!

The Spirit of Evil
A Meditation

❧

The Tempter

*T*hen Jesus was led into the desert by the spirit to be tempted by the devil. He fasted forty days and forty nights and afterward was hungry. The tempter approached and said to him, "If you are the Son of God, command these stones to turn into bread."

Jesus replied, "Scripture has it: Not on bread alone is man to live but on every utterance that comes from the *mouth of God."*

Next the devil took him to the holy city, set him on the parapet of the temple, and said, "If you are the Son of God, throw yourself down. Scripture has it: He will bid his angels take care of you; with their hands they will support you that you may never stumble on a stone."

Jesus answered him, "Scripture also has it: You shall not put the Lord your God to the test."

The devil then took him up a very high mountain and displayed before him all the kingdoms of the world in their magnificence, promising, "All these will I bestow on you if you prostrate yourself in homage before me."

At this Jesus said to him, "Away with you, Satan! Scripture has it: You shall do homage to the Lord your God; him alone shall you adore."

At that the devil left him, and angels came and waited on him.

(Matthew 4:1-11)

Chapter Five

❦

Original Sin

As we examine the sources of bad things that happen to people, we realize that not only is there something outside us in opposition to God, namely the devil, but there is something inside us as well. This is what we call Original Sin, our inner brokenness that often leads us to make poor choices.

A commentator once wisely observed that Original Sin is the

only doctrine of the Church that is empirically verifiable. In other words, we can't prove most of the doctrines of our creed using the scientific method. I can't prove the existence of God. I can't prove that there are three persons in God. I can't prove sanctifying grace. I believe all these, and I can give reasonable arguments for my belief, but I can't prove them from a scientific point of view.

However, we need only pick up the newspaper, watch television newscasts, listen to the radio in order to arrive at one conclusion: there is something terribly wrong with us humans. Every day the news is filled with stories of murders and rapes, thefts and cruelty, looking out for one's self and exploiting others. We see that human ability pervert nearly every effort at building a more just world. Part of us is building up, and another part of us is tearing down. This capacity to sabotage ourselves and each other is what I refer to as Original Sin.

Theologically, Original Sin goes back to Adam and Eve, to the sin of our first parents. There is something very human about that story. In essence God tells Adam and Eve that they can have the fruit of every tree in the garden but one. Naturally, they want the fruit of that one tree! Tell a child that he or she can have every toy but one, and he or she will naturally want that toy most. Suggest to parishioners that they not eat meat on Friday out of respect for the day Christ died, and that will naturally be the day when they want meat most. A smoker trying to quit smoking can think of nothing else but smoking!

A pundit once observed that the source of Original Sin was not the apple in the tree, but the pair on the ground! Whatever the choice was, our "first parents" made the wrong choice!

A very humble and holy lady once said to me, "I always

thought of the scene in the Garden of Eden as God saying, "Look, you can do it my way or you can try to live without me." Our first parents chose to do it their way!

And we inherit that brokenness. It's sort of in our genes! Even the best among us like St. Paul could complain of doing the things he did not want to do and not doing the things he wanted to do. He knew the inner struggle with his inner brokenness.

If we couple our inner brokenness with what we said in the last chapter about the devil, then a clearer picture of where death and tragedy come from begins to emerge. If the spirit of evil tempts us to drive too fast, there is a part of us willing to cooperate with the temptation. If the fallen angel of darkness appeals to our laziness in not replacing the brakes on a bus, there is a part of us willing to cooperate with that temptation. If there is an appeal to an engineer to save money by not designing the best road, there is a part of that person tempted by greed.

There can be an unholy alliance between the Father of Lies and our own inner brokenness.

Then, if we step back from individual acts, imagine the cumulative effects of Original Sin.

Look at the cumulative effects of poor choices that lead to pollution and famine and war. How often have terrible atrocities been perpetrated because thousands of people said the same kinds of things: "I was just following orders." "If I hadn't killed him, I would have been killed." "I've got to look out for my own family and loved ones."

Again, just look at those sentences. On one level, there is surely nothing wrong with obedience to a superior, with self-defense, with looking out for the best interests of your family or loved ones. Yet, historically, the Father of Lies has so managed to pervert the truth that we humans have been willing to cooperate in those perversions.

All those sentences spoken above have been used to make possible the Nazi concentration camps and the extermination of Jews and other groups. "I was just following orders." They have been used to explain the slaughter in Rwanda and the war lords inflicting famine on Somalia. They have been used to defend ethnic cleansing in various places. "If I hadn't killed, I would have been killed." "I've got to look out for my family and loved ones."

Even further, the cumulative effects of Original Sin become

abundantly clear in health issues. Suppose, for example, that world governments had not felt the need to use the best minds of its citizens on weapons of war. Suppose all that time and money and genius had been spent curing cancer and heart disease.

Surely, had all human energy been focused on goodness, we would have fewer child deaths, no famines, no wars. We would all be living much longer; we might even have colonized some of the planets by now.

So, despite being tempted to blame death and sickness and tragedy on God, we have no further to look than ourselves. It is not God's will. It is our will.

And surely the height of our capacity to cooperate with the darkness came when we cooperated in the crucifixion of our God.

Tragically, in times past, the death of Jesus on the cross was used to justify anti-Semitism. In reality, only fear and prejudice could lead to blaming Jews for the death of Jesus. Yes, some of the leaders of the Jews did plot the death of Jesus, and some of the fickle crowds did participate in cheering that on.

But what sense would it be to be anti-Jew when Jesus, God-made-

man, was a Jew! His first followers, the founders of our Christian
faith, were Jews. Many in the
crowds who followed him re-
mained loyal, and many of the
Jewish leaders did not endorse
putting him to death. Even in the
Scriptures there is noted the term,
"Jews who killed Jesus" to distin-
guish them from those who
would have nothing to do with
the death of that just man.

The deeper issue of the Scriptures
is that we all share responsibility
for the death of God. Every time
we fail to see the image and likeness of God in each other, we fail
to see God. Every time an innocent person dies needlessly, we

have again crucified the presence of God!

All prejudice is simply another face of Original Sin, the brokenness in us that would view others with fear and anger, that would make "them" wrong in order to make ourselves "right." How tragic it is that we would allow our national identity, our tribal identity, our gang identity to destroy other innocent people.

How tragic it is that after all these years of human history, we have yet to acknowledge the dignity and worth of each individual and our collective dignity and worth as members of the same human family, members of the same family created by God. Yet, that is a statement of unity and peace and the spirit of evil thrives on division and strife. Unfortunately, we are too often more prepared to cooperate with evil than with good.

Between the devil and Original Sin then, virtually all the terrors and tragedies of life can be explained. But there is still more.

Original Sin
A Meditation

∾

The First Story

*N*ow the serpent was the most cunning of all the animals that the Lord God had made. The serpent asked the woman, "Did God really tell you not to eat from any of the trees in the garden?"

The woman answered the serpent, "We may eat of the fruit of the trees in the garden. It is only about the fruit of the tree in the middle of the garden that God said, 'you shall not

*eat it or even touch it, lest you die.'"
But the serpent said to the woman,
"You certainly will not die! No, God
knows well that the moment you eat
of it you will be like gods who know
what is good and what is bad."*

*The woman saw that the tree was
good for food, pleasing to the eyes,
and desirable for gaining wisdom. So
she took some of its fruit and ate it;
and she also gave some to her husband, who was with her, and he ate
it.*

*Then the eyes of both of them were
opened, and they realized that they
were naked; so they sewed fig leaves
together and made loincloths for
themselves.*

When they heard the sound of the Lord God moving about in the garden at the breezy time of the day, the man and his wife hid themselves from the Lord God among the trees of the garden. The Lord God then called to the man and asked him, "Where are you?"

Adam answered, "I heard you in the garden but I was afraid, because I was naked, so I hid myself."

Then he asked, "Who told you that you were naked? You have eaten, then, from the tree of which I had forbidden you to eat!"

The man replied, "The woman whom you put here with me — she gave me fruit from the tree and so I ate it."

The Lord God then asked the woman, "Why did you do such a thing?"

The woman answered, "The serpent tricked me into it, so I ate it."

Then the Lord God said to the serpent, "Because you have done this, you shall be banned from all the animals and from all the wild creatures. You shall crawl on your belly and you shall eat dirt all the days of your life. I will put enmity between you and the woman and between your offspring and hers. He will strike at your head while you strike at his heel."

To the woman he said, "I will intensify the pangs of your childbearing; you shall bring forth children in pain. Yet your urge shall be for your husband, and he shall be your master."

To the man he said, "Because you listened to your wife and ate from the tree which I had forbidden you to eat, cursed be the ground because of you! In toil you shall eat its yield all the days of your life. It shall bring forth thorns and thistles to you, as you eat the plants of the field. By the sweat of your face you shall get bread to eat, until you return to the ground from which you were taken. For you are dirt and to dirt you shall return."

(Genesis 3:1-19)

Chapter Six

∾

Free Will

Once we have acknowledged that God does not will destructive or hurtful events, we continue our search for the causes of death and sickness and pain. We have seen the devil as the number one cause. Next, we looked at Original Sin, the brokenness within us. Put simply, as Ruth Tiffany Barnhouse, Episcopal priest and psychiatrist, puts it, "Original Sin is that which makes it impossible to always make the right decision." The power to make decisions, the power to choose, is what we call "free will."

God, in creating us, loved us so much that he gave us the absolute power to choose, even to choose against him, even to choose to reject him!

Given the terrible devastation that humanity has wrought through our use of free will, there are those who ask why God would have given us free will, knowing in advance, as God, some of the terrible ways we would use it? I surrender that question to the mystery of love. If you love someone, you have to give them freedom.

For God to create human beings, for God to create us in his own image and likeness, freedom had to be part of the package. No doubt, God could have chosen a different kind of creation — robots or automatons or some other type of creature.

The animal creation and the lower species seem more like that. They rely on instinct rather than thinking and knowledge. As someone put it, "Animals are conscious, but only humans are aware that we are conscious." To be human is to be free, to share this quality of divinity.

Perhaps if we looked at it from a humbler point of view, from our point of view, could we give meaningful life to our children without also giving them freedom?

True, you could guarantee that they would never be injured in a bus accident by locking them in a room all their lives, but what kind of life would that be? You could guarantee that they would never even stub a toe if you tied them to their beds, but what kind of life would that be?

In short, human life, which requires awareness, decision-making, and being responsible for the consequences of our decisions, necessarily involves free will.

Free will is capable of being manipulated. We have already spoken of the devil as the great tempter. We know that Original Sin will incline us to not always make the right decision.

Consequently, given the freedom we have, we will often make wrong decisions. There will always be consequences of such decisions. War, famine, pestilence, drug lords, drug dealers, drug users, liars, thieves, murderers, and on and on are all consequences of our choices.

As we know from studies of addiction (particularly Dr. Gerald May's book *Addiction and Grace*), repeated actions literally form "paths" in our brains, sequences of neurological and chemical reactions. Repeated patterns of behavior make it more and more difficult to behave otherwise.

As anyone who has ever tried to break an addiction can testify, it is often sheer hell for some period of time. For many, the addiction is physical as well as psychological.

But, however small, there is always a window of freedom. Despite pain so intense that it nearly maddens us, we can choose to not

take a drink, to not smoke the
next cigarette, to not do the next
drug. In short, there is always
hope because there is always
God! In a later chapter I will discuss the presence of God, and I
will argue that one of the places
God always resides is within us.

Ironically, one of the break-
through realities of AA, an orga-
nization that helps people to
break the addiction of alcohol,
was the discovery of the power of
altruism. To put it simply, I can
only finally and ultimately end
my addiction to some drug, by replacing it with altruism, the desire to help you end your
addiction.

As one man put it, "For years, I couldn't stop drinking because I always felt that the doctor or professional who was offering help was well and I was the sick one. I always felt so ashamed and weak asking for help. But when I joined AA, I discovered that if I needed to call a fellow-alcoholic at 3:00 a.m., I was actually helping him stay sober by asking for help for myself."

The irony is that we find our freedom only by surrendering to God. We replace an addiction to some chemical only by becoming "addicted" to helping others. In short, when we use our freedom to love the way God loves us, we become our best self and become truly free. When we allow the devil to dictate our agenda, when our brokenness believes his lies, then we split off, blame others, isolate ourselves from loving and being loved — and stay prisoners of the darkness.

But there is always hope because there is always God.

Free Will
A Meditation

❧

My Autobiography in
Five Short Chapters
by Portia Nelson

Chapter One
  I walk down the street.
  There is a deep hole in the
    sidewalk.
  I fall in
  I am lost ... I am helpless.
  It's not my fault.
  It takes forever to find a way
    out.

Chapter Two

I walk down the same street
There is a deep hole in the
  sidewalk.
I pretend I don't see it.
I fall in again.
I can't believe I am in the same
  place
But it isn't my fault.
It takes a long time to get out.

Chapter Three

I walk down the same street.
There is a deep hole in the
  sidewalk.
I see it there.
I still fall in ... it's a habit.
My eyes are open
I know where I am
It is my fault.
I get out immediately.

Chapter Four
I walk down the same street.
There is a deep hole in the
  sidewalk.
I walk around it.

Chapter Five
I walk down another street.

Chapter Seven

∾

The Forces of Nature

As we continue to examine the "circumstances" that alter God's *intentional will* for good, we come to a less precise area. The devil as a force of chaos and darkness is a fairly familiar concept to grasp, even if we cannot fully comprehend all the intricacies of evil. Original Sin as a sort of internal brokenness that we inherit from our first parents is a bit more complicated but still basically understandable. Free will is pretty cut and dried: we have the power to choose good or evil. The forces of nature are not quite as easy to understand.

For the sake of clarity let me just state that I will look at the forces of nature under two headings:

> 1) *The forces of nature that reflect the chaos that comes from the split between God and his creatures and his creation,* and

> 2) *The forces of nature that represent the laws for the good order of the world. (Gravity, for example, is a pretty good law. It keeps us from flying off into outer space!)*

Let's look at these separately. First, there are the forces of nature that reflect the chaos that works against the good order of God. At the beginning of the Bible, God is pictured as "brooding over a formless void" and basically bringing order out of the chaos. Creation occurred when God basically brought meaningful life into existence. Chaos and darkness were scattered.

However, after the fall of Adam and Eve, after the relationship between God and his creatures had been broken, there also seemed to be a break between God and his creation.

If you recall the creation story, women would bear children in pain and men would have to fight briars and thorns in raising crops. The implication is that had there been no sin, there would have been no pain in childbearing or in raising crops.

Again, it seems to hint at my basic understanding that the *intentional will* of God was only for good. God not only gave life but gave a wonderful life where creation would serve men and women without toil or violence.

Note too that after the Fall, murder and more violence entered the world. Finally, the flood destroyed humanity, and God built a new world with Noah and his descendants.

Rather than assuming the flood was caused by God, could we not assume that the flood was a result of the broken creation, of the power of chaos to destroy life, a power that God fights against?

God warns the people of the coming flood! Although only Noah and his family "hear" the warning, the problem is not with God. God is again and always on the side of life, even battling the forces of nature that seek to destroy his creation.

One of the greatest difficulties we face as believers is in understanding the Bible. The Bible is not just a book that fell from heaven, but it is a composite of many books that were written over thousands of years. From the earliest days of Abraham and Moses, the stories of God were passed on orally around the campfires. Once the kingdoms of David and Solomon were established, there was "leisure" time to write the stories and traditions down.

Consequently, what we see in the Hebrew Scriptures — what we have commonly called as Christians, the Old Testament — is an evolution of thought. From the earliest days God's will is often pictured as a cruel will. As someone said, "Cruel times create a cruel God."

With the sense of being God's chosen people and being promised a special land, the Hebrews assumed that God's will would be for them to kill the current occupants of that land! We would not imagine God that way today, but a more primitive understanding of God would have a less sophisticated image of God.

For example, when I see verses in the psalms that read, "For he smashes the children's heads against the rocks, for his mercy endures forever," I'm inclined to think that is not an accurate picture of God! Such "mercy" would be good news for one people, but not for others.

However, if you were part of a primitive tribe at war with other primitive tribes, it would make sense to slaughter the "little enemies" before they grew up and became "big enemies."

Again, as I mentioned earlier in this book, when God's chosen people believed that whatever happened was under God's control, then a successful slaughter of the enemy must also have been God's will.

However, by the time the Wisdom Books of the Bible were written, closer to the time of Jesus, we see an astounding verse from the Book of Wisdom:

"For God did not create death, nor does God rejoice in the destruction of the living, but by the envy of the devil, death entered the world... ."

What a difference. Being in a different place in their history, the Jews could begin to see God, not as a God wanting death but as a God wanting life. Now the devil was clearly seen as the perpetrator of death, not God.

Why am I making what seems like a long digression in this chapter about nature? Because

we need to see that our understanding of God is evolving just
as our understanding of virtually
everything else in life evolves.
God stays God, but our understanding of God changes.

When Jesus arrived on the scene,
he would preach a God so loving
that not only was killing condemned but giving of self was ex-
tolled.

He spoke of such profound trust
in the Father's goodness that we
could turn the other cheek, give
more than someone asked of us,
and even be killed and still be
okay!

What a change! From an understanding of God who asked us to
kill, to an understanding of God
who did not even tell us to defend ourselves! God was now so
clearly identified with love that
no form of hurt or death could be
inflicted in God's name.

Just, then, as there is a changing
understanding of God reflected
in the Bible, so there is a varied
understanding of nature reflected
in the Bible. To put it simply, the
world created by God is good.
The world that is in the hands of
"the evil one" is bad.

In St. John's Gospel, "the world"
is presented as those forces hos-

tile to Jesus. "Do not be surprised if the world hates you; it hated me before you," Jesus said. In the book of Job, the devil is portrayed as "patrolling the earth," implying that the earth was under his control. In the temptation scene, when Satan confronts Jesus, the world "and its kingdoms" do seem to be in the power of Satan.

However, Jesus also refers to the birds of the sky, to the regular changes of seasons, to his Father's "allowing the rain to fall on the good and the bad alike." Jesus speaks of the world as being under God's control.

Consequently, the two distinctions I made at the beginning of this chapter hold true. First, there is the world that represents the chaos, the world that is hostile to God. Here is where I put the hurricanes and tornadoes and earthquakes. Surely they are not God's will. They are part of the circumstances of life that attack and destroy life.

Second, however, are the forces of nature that serve God. Here I simply mean the laws that govern the seasons, the growing of crops, the raising of animals, the laws of mathematics and gravity. These are the laws that reflect the order of God.

However — and this is a *big* however — even these laws can be a source of destruction. Let's take gravity as an example. Gravity is wonderful. It means apples fall to the ground. It means oranges fall to the ground. It means bananas fall to the ground. We get all these wonderful fruits.

However, gravity also means that planes fall to the ground, if they should lose power. "An object in motion will continue in motion in a straight line unless... ." Thus even a good law can have disastrous effects.

However, we need to see God as respecting his own creation, not God wanting the plane to crash, not God swatting the plane out of the air for some reason.

Yes, God does work miracles on occasion, that is, God goes above and beyond the laws of nature. God, the creator of nature, surely has the power to contravene nature.

However, just as the miracles of Jesus were signs of a deeper healing and conversion of the spirit so the rare miracles of today are meant for our encouragement, not our expectation.

As a wise visitor from the East once commented when he observed the way Americans prayed, "In your culture it is considered a miracle when God does man's will. In my culture it is considered a miracle when man does God's will."

As we look back at the miracles of Jesus, his calming the winds and waves, for example, we see a symbol of God's recreating the world, restoring his order to the chaos. When we look at the many people Jesus healed physically in his day, we realize that none of them are still alive.

Apparently, because of our brokenness, the human body just won't last forever. The real miracle Jesus worked, then, was what he did for their spirits. We believe the spirits of those Jesus healed are alive today with God.

In saying all that I have said about God in this chapter I want to re-emphasize that God does not change, but our awareness and understanding of God does change. None of us can know all there is to know about God in a lifetime, or a century, or even a millennium. God is infinite; we humans remain finite.

However, when the fullness of God was revealed in Jesus, the essence of God was also revealed. God is love. It will take forever to fully comprehend what "God is love" truly means. What it means in the context of this book is that God will always be on our side against the forces of darkness...

helping us resist the wiles
of the devil,
helping us heal our brokenness,
strengthening us to make wise
choices,
helping us to appreciate
nature even while its chaos
resists God and its order
reveals God.

Sin, darkness, death, and disease
will not prevail. God will prevail.
And the resurrection of the body
is the ultimate triumph of God
over the power of nature.

The Forces of Nature
A Meditation

∿

Four Engines or Four Priests

*T*he story is told of a plane that had a fire in one of its four engines. Immediately, the pilot came on the air and announced that there was a fire in one of the engines; but not to worry, there were four engines and the three that were working would be more than enough to get them to their destination safely.

Then, to further reassure the passengers, he announced, "In case any of *you are still worried, I want you to know that we have four priests on this flight. So you have nothing to worry about."*

Just then, a little old lady's voice could be heard from the back of the plane saying, "I'd rather have four engines than four priests."

Section Three

❧

Where Is God?

Chapter Eight

∾

God the Nurturing Parent—Providence

Having established that God intends only good for us and that the circumstances of life — the devil, Original Sin, free will, and the forces of nature — can create the tragedies of life, we are now forced to face another ultimate question:

Where is God when the tragedy happens?

Where is God when the baby dies, when the famine occurs? Where is he when I am faced with the losses of separation and divorce and death?

Since as Christians we believe in a Trinity — three persons in one God — then I believe that God is in three places:

God the Father is the God above us, looking out for us, which we call Providence.

God the Son, Jesus, is the God who suffers with us, which we call Compassion.

God the Holy Spirit is the God within us, which we call Grace.

I'll devote the next two chapters to the second two members of the Trinity. This chapter will be devoted to God the Father, God the nurturing parent.

Naming God as Father is the traditional, credal statement of our understanding of God. However, in the book of Genesis when God creates humans, God creates them "in the image and likeness of God, male and female God created them." Obviously, then, if male and female are the image of

God, there must be both the masculine and the feminine within God!

Consequently, we could probably refer to God as both Father and Mother. The term nurturing parent is how I titled this chapter. It captures the sense of God as a parent, looking out for children, vitally involved in caring for them.

When I refer to God throughout this book in the masculine, in the form that credal statements refer to God, I obviously include the possibility of the more inclusive understanding of God.

Where is God when tragedy happens? God is the Father, apart from us but still caring about us. God is transcendent, that is, above us. The transcendent God has been referred to as the "God outside our human realm of distortions and lies and not able to be controlled by them."

God the Father is separate from us, separate from being controlled by the powers of evil but still caring for us, much as a parent in the United States is separate from a child working in China, but is still vitally caring about the child's life.

Jesus said, "The sparrow does not fall to the earth without the Father's noticing it. Are you not worth more than many sparrows?"

The Father has sent his Son, has given his Spirit, and continues to encourage, to inspire, to draw all things to himself through his Son. The Father sees how his intention for good is altered by the power of evil, but the Father will not let evil prevail. When darkness seems to have won, when evil seems to have triumphed, when we lie dead, seemingly defeated, the Father will raise us up just as he raised his son up!

The power of the Father is the ultimate power of life over death. The resurrection of the body is the ultimate and eternal miracle. The circumstances of life can alter and delay the intentions of the Father for good, but darkness and death will not prevail.

When evil closes the window, God will open the door. When sin seems to have triumphed, God the Father will forgive the sin. When death seems victorious, God will see that life triumphs. God the Father wills good for us, and good will prevail — if not in this life, surely in the next.

God the Nurturing Parent
A Meditation

∾

from *Life of the Balanced*
by Father Henri Nouwen

*L*ong before any human being sees
us, God sees us with his loving
eyes. Long before anyone hears us cry
or laugh, God, who is all ears for us,
hears us. Long before any person
speaks to us in this world, we are
spoken to by the voice of eternal love.

Our precariousness, uniqueness, and
individuality are not given to us by

those who meet us in clock time (our brief chronological existence) but by one who has chosen us with an ever-lasting love, a love that existed from all eternity and will last through all eternity.

The truth is that I am the chosen child of God, precious in God's eyes, called the beloved from all eternity and held safe in an everlasting em-brace. That is the truth of our lives. That is the truth spoken by the voice that says, "You are my beloved."

Listening to that voice with great in-ner attentiveness, I hear at my center words that say, "I have called you by name, from the very beginning. You are mine, and I am yours. You are my beloved; on you my favor rests. I have molded you in the depths of the earth and knitted you together in your mother's womb. I have carved you in the palms of my hands and hidden you in the shadow of my embrace.

"I look at you with infinite tenderness and care, a care more intimate than that of a mother for her child. I have counted every hair on your head and guided you at every step. Wherever you go, I go with you; and wherever you rest, I keep watch.

"I will give you food that will satisfy all your hunger and drink that will quench all your thirst. I will not hide my face from you. You know me as your own as I know you as my own. You belong to me. I am your father, your mother, your brother, your sis-

ter, your love, your spouse ... yes, even your child ... wherever you are, I will be. Nothing will ever separate us. We are one."

Chapter Nine

∾

God the Son, God With Us— Compassion

As we ponder where God is when tragedy strikes, we have seen God the Father, the one who watches over us, Divine Providence, the one who will not allow even death to contain us.

As we look at Jesus, the second person of the Trinity, we see God-with-us, Emmanuel. If we could only visualize God as transcendent, as above and beyond us, we might well feel abandoned.

A popular song years ago sang of God watching "from a distance." Jesus is the God who took away the distance between humans and God! He took on flesh and blood and became one with us to show us that God was not afraid to get hurt to tell us how much he loved us!

For many of us the sense of God's becoming one with us seems far away and long ago. But that's not so. Yes, the historical life of Jesus of Nazareth did take place two thousand years ago. The historical Jesus of Nazareth could only be in one place at one time.

However, the resurrected and glorified Jesus, the Jesus who is Lord of history, is not so confined. In the Scriptures and throughout Christian tradition, we are seen as the Body of Christ with Christ as our Head. The head cannot be separate from the body. The concerns and pains and fears of the body continue to be the concern of the head as well.

Perhaps this is best brought home in the dramatic scene in the Acts of the Apostles when Paul was converted on the way to Damascus. The voice that spoke out of the blinding light said, "Saul, Saul, why are you persecuting me?"

Note the word "me"! Jesus does not say, "why are you persecuting those people, those Christians, those individuals?" He says "me" to bring home the point that God never leaves his people.

This is our compassionate God. The word "compassion" comes from two Latin words which together mean "suffer with." Jesus is the one who came to suffer with us. Jesus continues to identify with us and suffer with us. Our pains and tragedies and losses are not "at a distance."

How does this work? Again it is a mystery of love. And yet, quantum physics has pointed out the interconnectedness of all reality. And theologians speak of God's giving his name to Moses in the burning bush as "I Am." God is the "eternal now." For us humans, life is lived with a past, a present, and a future.

But for God, all of time is present time. So while the crucifixion of Christ is indeed past time, and Christ suffers that event no more, Christ does continue to identify in the present with our crucifixions and betrayals and pains.

How does this presence look practically? It looks like us! Any

time I have ever buried a child or
a person killed tragically, the fu-
neral home or church is always
packed with people! Total
strangers turn out to offer sympa-
thy and help.

Where is God when the child or
parent or spouse dies? Right next
to the bereaved person in the persons of all those people! There is
God holding the bereaved person
while he or she cries. There is
God bringing food to the family.
There is God offering to watch
the children or drive a loved one
home.

We humans seem so reluctant to
get the message that we are creat-

ed "in the image and likeness of God." When we reach out to each other in love, we reveal the face of God! As one of the hymns goes, "God has no hands now but yours. No arms now but yours."

We become the way God gets into the world.

The problem with so much of the mystery of suffering is that we struggle with the mystery of life. We keep looking for God somewhere else. The people who missed God the first time around in human history were looking for God somewhere else.

They didn't expect to see God in swaddling clothes as a baby in a manger.

They didn't expect to see God as a carpenter.

They didn't expect to see God as an itinerant preacher.

They didn't expect a God who would suffer and die.

This is not said to condemn them.

We are no different from them. We keep looking for God to work some miracle coming out of the clouds, and we forget that God wants to work a greater miracle of love by coming out of us!

The God who stays with us is our reminder and model of how to stay with each other. Love can bring a person back from the depth of depression, back from the graves of our fears, back from despair to hope. Yes, God is separate from us with powers that transcend us, but God in his Son is present with us, giving us the same power that Jesus had, namely the power to love.

Where is God?

As close as the closest person who loves you genuinely and unconditionally.

God the Son
A Meditation

❧

Footprints

*O*ne day a man had a dream. He dreamed he was walking along the beach with the Lord.

Across the sky flashed scenes from his life. For each scene he noted two sets of footprints in the sand: one belonging to him and the other to the Lord.

When the last scene of his life flashed before him, he looked at the footprints in the sand. He noticed that many times along the path of his life, there was only one set of footprints. He also noticed that it happened at the very lowest and saddest times in his life.

This observation bothered him, and he asked the Lord about it.

"Lord, you said that once I decided to follow you, you'd walk with me all the way. But I have noticed that during the most troublesome times of my life, there is only one set of footprints. I don't understand why, when I needed you most, you would abandon me."

The Lord replied, "My child, I love you. I would never leave you. Dur-

ing the times of trial and suffering, when you see only one set of foot-prints, it was I who carried you!"

Chapter Ten

❧

God the Holy Spirit, God In Us-Grace

Where is God in our moments of pain? We have named two places where God is. First, God is above us, looking out for us, even defeating death to save us. Second, there is the Son, God-with-us, sharing our pain, suffering with us, comforting us. Finally, where is God? God is Spirit. God is within each of us.

There's a whimsical parable about the smartest man in the world, a man so smart that even God consulted him from time to time!

One day God said to the man, "I want to play a game of hide and seek with humanity. Where can I hide that people will never find me?"

The wisest man in the world responded, "Hide in the human heart. They'll never think to look for you there."

This was the message Jesus preached again and again:

"I will give you another Para-
clete, the Spirit."

"The kingdom of God is within
you."

In our moments of greatest
tragedy, it is the Father above us
sustaining us, the Son with us
supporting us, and God within us
strengthening us. The God within
is what we call grace — the sanctifying grace of God's presence
and the actual grace of God's
strength!

Dr. Anne Kaiser Stearns in her
book *Triumphant Survivors* traces
three types of people who have
had significant losses in their
lives.

The first group she studied are people who never get over the loss. They define their lives by the loss.

A second group recovers from the loss and bounces back to where they were before the loss.

A third group, however, the group she names the "triumphant survivors," not only bounce back but manage to come back better people than they were before the loss.

The founder of MADD, Mothers Against Drunk Drivers, would be an example of a triumphant survivor. This woman who lost a child to a drunk driver used her anger and pain to form a nation-wide group that has doubtless saved the lives of hundreds and thousands of other teenagers. Instead of withdrawing into a pained depression, she used her pain as a reason to reach out to help others.

This Spirit that motivated her to create something to save the lives of others is, I believe, the work of grace, the work of God within her. The grace, the presence of God, is available to all, but due to our inner brokenness, not all of us will respond to God's presence. Even the presence of God within us will not take away our free will.

Another example of a triumphant survivor is Everett Alvarez. Everett Alvarez is the longest survivor of a North Vietnamese prison camp. He spent eight and a half years there: caged, often beaten, poorly fed and clothed.

Alvarez, when asked how he managed to survive the confinement and degradation for that long, responded, "I could not take it a day at a time. A day at a time was much too long. I took it a minute at a time. I can survive this torture one more minute. I can survive this prison one more minute. I can survive this mental anguish one more minute."

Alvarez went on to comment that we never know what we can endure until we are tested.

That enduring spirit, I believe, is the Spirit of God within.

I know another true story of a man whose daughter had been raped by a gang as she went to work as a nurse at an inner-city hospital. The girl never got over the trauma and eventually committed suicide. The father then went to visit the men in prison who had raped his daughter and forgave them! Family and friends were angered and dismayed.

"How could you do that?" they
demanded.

He responded simply, "They had
taken my daughter's life. I cannot
bring her back. But if I carried all
that anger and bitterness within
me for the rest of my life, they
would have taken my life too."

The tragedies and injustices of
life are real. The victims are many.
But God is real, and God is good.
God remains with us: above us,
beside us, and within us.

The powers of evil can degrade
our bodies, attack our minds, and
attempt to obliterate even our
flesh. But we have a God who
loves the very dust we return to.

Just as we are at our best when we love each other and see the image of God in each other, so too God looks at us and sees his own image. How could God ever forget his own image, his own reflection, his own children?

Father Andrew Greeley has wisely observed that salvation in history is really the story of a God who fell in love with his own creatures. You never forget someone you have loved.

God the Holy Spirit
A Meditation

✑

The Strength of God's Love

*A*re they Hebrews? So am I! Are
they Israelites? So am I! Are
they seed of Abraham? So am I! Are
they ministers of Christ? Now I am
really talking like a fool. I am more
with my many more labors and im-
prisonments, with far worse beatings
and frequent brushes with death.

Five times I received forty lashes less
one; three times I was beaten with
rods; I was stoned once, shipwrecked

three times; I passed a day and a night on the sea.

I traveled continually, endangered by floods, robbers, my own people, the Gentiles; imperiled in the city, in the desert, at sea, by false brothers; enduring labor, hardship, many sleepless nights; in hunger and thirst and frequent fasting, in cold and nakedness. Leaving other suffering unmentioned, there is that daily tension pressing on me, my anxiety for all the churches... .

As to the extraordinary revelations, in order that I might not become conceited, I was given a thorn in the flesh, an angel of Satan to beat me and keep me from getting proud.

Three times I begged the Lord that this might leave me.

He said to me, "My grace is enough for you; for in weakness, power reaches perfection." And so I willingly boast of my weakness instead, that the power of Christ might rest upon me.

Therefore I am content with weakness, with mistreatment, with distress, with persecutions and difficulties for the sake of Christ; for when I am powerless, it is then that I am strong.

(II Corinthians 11:22-28; 12:7-10)

God the Holy Spirit
A Meditation

∽

Dying

*O*nce upon a time, twin boys were conceived. When each perceived the life of the other and his own life, they knew that life was good and they laughed and rejoiced.

One said, "We're lucky to have been conceived in this world."

The other said, "Blessed be the mother who gave us this life."

They grew and explored their womb world. They found the cord that gave them life from the mother's blood. They sang her praises. "How great is the mother who shares all she has with us."

Weeks passed and they grew and changed. One of them wondered aloud, "We're changing. What can it mean?"

"We're drawing near to birth," the other replied.

They were afraid because they knew that birth meant leaving their world behind.

"If it were up to me, I'd stay here forever," one of the twins said.

"We have to be born. It has happened to all others before us." For there was evidence of life before them, as the mother had borne others.

"But is there life after birth?" one asked. *"How can there be life after birth? Don't we shed our life cord and also our blood tissues? Have you ever talked to anyone who has been born? Has anyone ever returned to the womb after birth? If the purpose of conception and all our growth is ended in birth, then truly life is absurd."*

Resigned to despair, the first twin concluded, *"If this is so and life is absurd, then there can really be no mother."*

"But there is a mother. Who else gave us nourishment and our world?" the other responded.

"We get our own nourishment, and our world has always been here. If there is a mother, who is she? Have you ever seen her or talked to her? No. We invented the notion of mother because it satisfied a need in us. It made us secure and happy."

So while one raved and despaired, the other resigned himself to birth and placed his trust in the hands of the mother, and together they feared what they did not know.

Days and weeks passed, and it came to be that they were born into light. They coughed out fluid and gasped *the dry air, and when they were sure that they had been born, they opened their eyes, seeing for the first time. They lay open-mouthed and awestruck before the great beauty and truth they could not hope to have known. They found themselves cradled in the warm love of their mother!*

❧ *Conclusion* ❧

And so there you have it. To summarize: God intends only good. The circumstances of life can bend and twist God's good intentions, but ultimately God prevails. We can indeed "let go and let God" in the sense of having absolute trust that God's goodness will prevail.

What are the circumstances that bend and twist God's good intentions? As I have noted, they are four: first, the spirit of evil that works against us from the outside; second, Original Sin — our

inner brokenness; third, free will
— our power to choose, to make
bad choices as well as good; and
the fourth, forces of nature.

Where is God when these "circumstances" are doing their
worst? There is God the Father,
God above us, guiding us with
his providence and even calling
us back from the dust when evil
and death have done their worst.
There is God the Son, Jesus, the
compassionate God still suffering
with his people. Third, there is
God the Holy Spirit, God within
us, helping us to endure and triumph over the powers of sin,
death, and darkness.

All of this is just another way of saying that God truly is Emmanuel — "God with us," not God against us.

We come from the hand of God, and we return to the hand of God, and God accompanies us on our journey. When a lady who was divorced, working full time, and going to school was asked how she did it all, she responded simply, "God puts angels on my path." Angels are both messengers and signs of the presence of God.

Life on this planet is not always fair. But the God of eternity is eternally fair, and God stays faithful to a faithful people:

"You shall seek the Lord, your God, and you shall indeed find him when you search after him with your whole heart and whole soul. In your distress, when all these things shall come upon you, you shall finally return to the Lord, your God, and heed his voice.

"Since the Lord, your God, is a merciful God, he will not abandon and destroy you, not forget the covenant which under oath he made with your fathers."

(Deuteronomy 4:29-31)

Addenda

1 From the pastoral constitution on the Church in the modern world of the Second Vatican Council (Gaudium et Spes, nn 18, 22):

In the face of death the enigma of human existence reaches its climax. Man is not only the victim of pain and the progressive deterioration of his body; he is also, and more deeply, tormented by the fear of final extinction. But the instinctive judgment of his heart is right when he shrinks from, and rejects, the idea of a total collapse and definitive end of his own person. He carries within him the seed of eternity, which cannot be reduced to matter alone, and so he rebels against death. All efforts of technology, however useful they may be, cannot calm his anxieties; the biological extension of his life-span cannot satisfy the desire inescapably present in his heart for a life beyond this life.

Imagination is completely helpless when confronted by death. Yet the Church, instructed by divine revelation, affirms that man has been created by God for a destiny of happiness beyond the reach of earthly trials. Moreover, the Christian faith teaches that bodily death, to which man would not have been subject if he had not sinned, will be conquered, the almighty and merciful Savior will restore man to the wholeness that he had lost through his own fault. God has called man, and still calls him, to be united in his whole being in perpetual communion with himself in the immortality of the divine life. This victory has been gained for us by the risen Christ, who by his own death has freed men from death.

Faith, presented with solid arguments, offers every thinking person the answer to his questionings concerning his future destiny. At the same time, it enables him to be one in Christ with his loved ones who have been taken from him by death and gives him hope that they have entered into true life with God.

Certainly the Christian is faced with the necessity and the duty of fighting against evil through many trials and of undergoing death. But by entering into the paschal mystery and being made like Christ in death, he will look forward, strong in hope, to the resurrection.

This is true not only of Christians but also of all men of good will in whose hearts grace is invisibly at work. Since Christ died for all men, and the ultimate vocation of man is in fact one, that is, a divine vocation, we must hold that the Holy Spirit offers to all the possibility of being united with this paschal mystery in a way known only to God.

Such is the great mystery of man, enlightening believers through the Christian revelation. Through Christ and in Christ light is thrown on the enigma of pain and death which overwhelm us without his Gospel to teach us. Christ has risen, destroying death by his own death; he has given us the free gift of life so that as sons in the Son we may cry out in the Spirit saying: "Abba, Father!"

2 A question I have heard often these past few weeks is, "How is that young man with the brain tumors doing?" I can say today that Craig Warnick is fine. He is finally at home with God. On January 2, 1997, the life support equipment was removed at Johns

Hopkins Hospital, and surrounded by those he loved most, Craig left this world for a world where there "will be no tears or sorrow, no crying out or pain."

In his superb homily, Father Chris Whatley told the young people in the congregation at Sacred Heart in Glyndon that Craig was one of life's real heroes. Craig had been a superb student-athlete at Franklin Senior High School. He played basketball, soccer, and baseball.

He was on the same team with "Moose" Haas. Craig was considered by many a better athlete, being voted best All-Around Senior for the class of 1974. Moose went on to a Major League career. Craig went on to battle brain tumors for 22 years. Life is not always fair, but God is always fair.

Life's heroes, Father Whatley reminded us, are not those who attain fame in some field of sports, but those who can be forced to the bench, but who never give up on life. Craig has every reason to give up. But he never did, and that's what makes him a hero.

In his final "coherent" hours, Craig had been able to tell his wife Susan, that she had been his life, and, without her and his daughter, Chloe, he would have died much sooner.

Susan, as you may recall, was the beautiful teenager who fell in love with Craig in high school. When she was told to forget Craig by certain doctors, and even by some friends, her love never waivered.

When she was told that Craig would never walk again, she responded, "He will walk. He'll walk down the aisle and marry me." When she took Craig "for better, for worse, in sickness and in health," she meant it.

She stayed by his side for seventeen years of marriage, through endless brain tumor surgeries and rehabs, through countless

heartbreaks and disappointments. The world renowned neu-
rosurgeon, Dr. Ben Carson, said
that Craig and Susan had taught
him what married love was really
all about. Susan not only escorted
Craig down the aisle for their
wedding, but she escorted Craig
all the way to eternity.

It's difficult to estimate the number of lives that Craig touched.
The irony is that, in battling disease all of his adult life, he may
have influenced more people for
good than if he had been a successful athlete. Every life has
meaning. All pain can be redemptive.

A nurse in the neuro-intensive care unit at Hopkins Hospital said that in Craig's last days there was a steady stream of oncologists and urologists and ophthalmologists and various doctors from other specialties who stopped by his bed to pay their respects. Most told of how much they had come to love Craig, and almost all left with the words to the staff, "Take good care of him." The care-receiver had had an impact on the lives of many care-givers. No doubt thousands of patients will be treated more compassionately and more sensitively because of the life of Craig Warnick.

So, now, instead of praying for Craig, I encourage you to pray to

Craig. He is surely one of God's saints. As we all face sickness and disease, increased limitations and pain, we can find a ready support in the life of Craig Warnick. And, as you pray to Craig, don't forget to pray for Susan and Chloe. While they know that Craig's love and spirit will be with them always, the loss of his physical, tangible presence leaves a terrible void in their lives.

If you wish to do something tangible for them, Susan has set up a fund for her daughter's education. If you care to, you can send a contribution to The Chloe Warnick Education Fund, P.O. Box 4684, Timonium, MD 21094-4684.

Beyond all else, however, try to appreciate the meaning of Craig's "Gospel of Life." We live in a culture of death. If a pregnancy is inconvenient, the life of the fetus is aborted. If an elderly person's care is too expensive, the life is ended. People in pain want the "right" to die with dignity. The answer our society gives to many of life's complexities is simply death!

But Craig and Susan remind us that the answer is life. No life is a mistake. No pain is without meaning. We can face all of life's cruelties and challenges with courage and dignity. The answer is not to embrace death. The answer is to embrace Christ, and then depression, despair, and death lose their power to control us.

3 A final note on death from reading the Gospels with the church — From *Christmas Through Easter* by Father Raymond Brown S.S. (St. Anthony Messenger Press, 1996), pp 42-43.

Whether the death of a loved one or one's own death, it is the moment when one realizes that all depends on God. No human support goes with one to the grave: credit cards, health insurance, retirement programs, and human companionship stop at the tomb. One enters alone.

If there is no God, there is nothing; if Christ has not conquered death, there is no future. The brutality of that realization causes trembling even among those who have spent their lives professing Christ. It is not unusual for people to confess that doubts have come into their minds as they face death.

Paul cries out that death is the last enemy to be overcome (I Corinthians 15:26), an insight that John captures by placing the Lazarus story at the end of Jesus' public ministry. From it we learn that no matter how fervently catechumens or already baptized Christians make or renew a baptismal profession in Lent, they still face a moment when their faith will be tested.

It will be precisely at that moment, when we are confronted with the visible reality of the grave, that we need to hear and embrace the bold message that Jesus proclaims in John's Gospel, "I am the life." Despite all appearance to the contrary, "Everyone who believes in me shall never die at all."

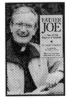